MINDFULLY INCLUSIVE

Connecting Social-Emotional Learning With Diversity, Equity, and Inclusion Skills

Teresa Cruz Foley, M Ed.

What's Inside

A SCIENTIFIC APPROACH

Behavioral Science maintains that **all behaviors serve a purpose and are maintained by consequences**.

- Adults can cause dysregulation in children. Our behavior can absolutely trigger maladaptive behavior in children. We're not bad people. Behavior science can help us do better.
    - Kids naturally match your intensity.
    - Shame increases maladaptive behavior.

The best thing I learned in grad school was the greeting at the door study. Greeting students by name as they walk in and saying one nice thing to them increased on-task productivity by 27%. [1]

You are highly encouraged to utilize this low-cost, high-yield strategy.
"Teachers with higher rates of general praise were found to report being more efficacious." [2]

Proven strategies to avoid power struggle:
- Explain changes to routine early and often.
- Listen and validate.
- Keep Yourself Regulated.
- Offer calming tools - stuffy, bean bag chair, music.
- Co-create the coping strategy.
    - Write down the answer to the question they repeat.
    - Create a visual schedule they can reference.

Noncontingent Reinforcement is a magical miracle.
- Give them what they love, often, on a schedule. Clinically proven to reduce problem behaviors. (Praise is the most effective and easiest.)
- It improves the relationship which improves behavior.
- PLEASE reinforce YOURSELF throughout the day. Your job is hard, and you're doing amazing.

In Conclusion:
- Understanding the function of the behavior helps us intervene more effectively.
- Always prioritize Reinforcing Positive Behaviors.
- When in doubt, take away demands and add more praise.
- Make it super easy at first to create momentum.
- Remember to Reward Yourself! This is hard! You're amazing! You'll do better for them if you reinforce yourself.

LESSON COMPONENTS

These lessons are designed to be highly versatile. Each component will take between 5 and 10 minutes depending on class size and participation. A component can stand alone or be split up as your day allows.

Connection
Connection asks a question related to the lesson's theme - You can go around the circle if you have time, or take a few raised hands. You can share first to set the stage for the level of sharing. Don't force participation. I have a rule during check-in that I have to answer their questions, they don't have to answer mine.

Discussion
Discussion gets deeper into the theme. It may involve a story, scenario, or relevant facts.

Practice
Practice involves physical integration of the lesson theme.

Breathwork will have detailed instructions. I've included an extensive list of breathwork practices in the back of this book. Once y'all have learned a few, if there's something you or the kids prefer to do than the one in the lesson plan - go for it.

Mindful Minute
1. Set the timer for 1 minute.
2. Y'all will close your eyes or focus on an object in the center and focus on taking normal breaths.
3. Minds will wander. When they do, silently congratulate yourself for recognizing, and gently bring attention back to your breath. (I am always nervous about introducing this but the kids surprise me every time with how well they take to it.)

Journal Activity
The writing/drawing prompts can be customized to different ages and ability levels. As long as students use journal time to write or draw, following the prompts isn't mandatory, as listening to their own intuition and desires is encouraged as it aligns with mindfulness practice.

Affirmation
An affirmation is a short, empowering sentence that sums up the lesson. You can have everyone repeat it together 3 times, and it can be written in a place where kids can see it all day.

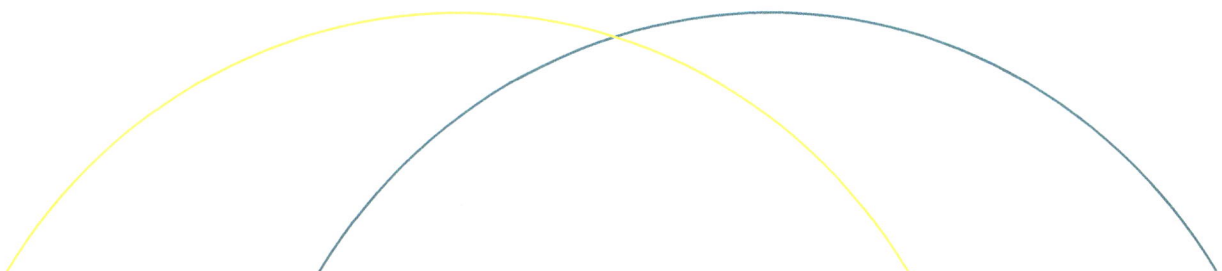

Section 1

Our Amazing Minds

Intro to Mindfulness
Chihuahua and Wise Owl
Emotions in Our Bodies

Lesson 1: Introduction to Mindfulness

Connection

Who has had an experience where something stressful happened and you couldn't stop thinking about it the whole day?

Discussion

Mindfulness is the ability to slow down what's happening in your head so you don't get carried away by it. We are going to learn many different mindfulness tools in this course. Mindfulness techniques have TONS of proven benefits. They have been linked to boosting recovery and immunity after injury or illness, reducing depression and anxiety, increasing happiness, improving coordination, improving creativity, boosting energy, and managing stress. Research shows that mindfulness practice reduces violence in prisons, improves grades for school children, and helps top athletes improve.

Who practices mindfulness?
Pro athletes
- **Serena Williams** meditates to stay calm under pressure.
- **Carli Lloyd**, FIFA World Cup and Olympic gold medal winner, meditates as part of her training routine. She visualizes what she wants to achieve to help her focus before games.
- **Lebron James** can be seen meditating in time-out sessions to get his mind in focus.
- **Kobe Bryant** said that meditation keeps his mind fast and focused in high-pressure situations.
- **Stephen Curry** uses visualization techniques to outsmart opponents. The Seattle Seahawk coach said that mindfulness techniques played a huge part in their Superbowl win of 2014

Industry Leaders
- **Steve Jobs**, the founder of Apple, inc. used meditation as a tool to expand his vision throughout the creation of his company.
- **George Lucas**, the creator of Star Wars, has been meditating for 40 years.
- **Oprah Winfrey** has hired teachers to lead her staff in meditation twice daily. She says "Meditation is a heightened state that lets whatever you're doing be your best life."

Musical superstars
- **Lady Gaga**, **Beyonce**, **Shawn Mendes**, **Camila Cabello**, and **Selena Gomez** all meditate. **Miley Cyrus** meditates before interviews to focus on her intentions, and **Lizzo** hosted a meditation on Instagram to help fans find calm during the COVID-19 pandemic.

Affirmation : *I can use mindfulness to be my best.*

Practice

Glitter jar activity

You'll need a mason jar filled with water, school glue, and glitter.

1. Fill half the jar with warm water, add 2 TBS glue, and stir.
2. Sprinkle in the glitter and share a story of a time you felt sad, scared, or angry.
3. Add room temperature water to almost full. Seal and shake.
4. As y'all watch the glitter settle, talk about how feelings can get shaken up, and as we become aware of our feelings, it's like having them settle so you can see and think clearly.

Mindful Minute

Put the jar in the center where everyone can see it.

1. Set a timer for 1 minute (I usually ask another adult to keep time).
2. Y'all will close your eyes or focus on an object in the center and focus on taking normal breaths.
3. Minds will wander. When they do, silently congratulate yourself for recognizing, and gently bring attention back to your breath. (I am always nervous about introducing this but the kids surprise me every time with how well they take to it.)

Journal Activity

Write/draw what you hope to get out of mindfulness training. Write as your future self about the benefits you've gained. Write or draw yourself doing something that calms you.

More room to doodle!

Journal Activity

Write/draw what you hope to get out of mindfulness training. Write as your future self about the benefits you've gained. Write or draw yourself doing something that calms you.

Lesson 2: Chihuahua Brain & Wise Owl

Connection

What do you tell yourself when your grown-up is late to pick you up? (Prompts - running late, will be here soon / accident / forgot about me / blame yourself - maybe I told them the wrong time).

How about when you are about to start a new school year or camp? What were some of the stories you tell yourself about what might happen? What other situations make you nervous?

Discussion

Cartoons, video games, and action movies all keep us on the edge of our seats. We experience so many threats in the virtual world, we can become used to feeling scared or anxious.

The amygdala is a tiny part of your brain that activates your stress response. Its job is to **watch for threats**. It's overactive in most of us, always barking like an angry Chihuahua. The pre-frontal cortex, your wise owl brain, activates your **relaxation, healing, and learning responses**. It's a good decision-maker, unlike the Chihuahua. When one of these is active, the other can't be. We can calm the Chihuahua and activate the wise owl by moving, singing, meditation, and other mindfulness practices.

Affirmation : *Wise owl brain, activate!*

Practice

Thoughts on Parade
Imagine you're watching a parade go by. Now imagine each of your thoughts as a float in the parade. You don't join the parade, you're just watching them pass. Just stand back and enjoy watching them pass on, knowing that even your biggest thoughts will go by.

Journal Activity

A very simple and powerful tool to help us calm down when we catastrophize is simply to recognize our anxious story and to say to ourselves, I'm having the thought that… or the story I'm telling myself is …

Write or draw an anxious thought. Then add the words, "I'm having the thought that…" or "I'm telling myself the story that…" If you're drawing, you can draw a thought bubble around the anxious scenario and draw yourself thinking about it.

More room to doodle!

Journal Activity

A very simple and powerful tool to help us calm down when we catastrophize is simply to recognize our anxious story and to say to ourselves, I'm having the thought that... or the story I'm telling myself is …

Write or draw an anxious thought. Then add the words, "I'm having the thought that…" or "I'm telling myself the story that…" If you're drawing, you can draw a thought bubble around the anxious scenario and draw yourself thinking about it.

Lesson 3: Emotions in Our Bodies

Connection

Share a personal example of a time when you were emotional or had a recurring emotion and where you feel it in your body. How do you feel when…

    a. You ace a test?
    b. Fun plans get canceled last minute?
    c. You have to sit in a car for 2 hours?
    d. Your grown-up is late to pick you up?
    e. You played great and your team won?

Discussion

Our emotions cause sensations in our bodies. Sometimes emotions take over our bodies, and we don't really feel in control. Somatics are how our emotions affect our physical bodies. Movement helps us take our power back from our emotions.

Affirmation : *Listening to my big feelings helps me calm down.*

Practice

Emotions Charade
Write 1 feeling word each on a small piece of paper.
- 1 person takes a piece of paper and strikes a pose to show that emotion.
- Everyone tries to guess the emotion
- Kids take turns acting out the emotion.

calm	confident	cranky	bored	worried
disappointed	embarrassed	excited	exhausted	frustrated
grateful	jealous	lonely	overwhelmed	panicked
refreshed	relieved	sad	relaxed	surprised

Box Breath
This is a very common breathwork practice that helps regulate emotions. Breathe in for 3 seconds. Hold for 3 seconds. Breath out for 3 seconds. Hold for 3 seconds. It's helpful if you count out loud while the students breathe. For variety you can increase the number of seconds for all sides of the box, or make the exhale longer than the rest.

Journal Activity
Journaling about our emotions is another great way to feel in control of them. Write or draw a recent time in your life when you felt a strong emotion. Where did you feel it in your body?

More room to doodle!

Journal Activity

Journaling about our emotions is another great way to feel in control of them. Write or draw a recent time in your life when you felt a strong emotion. Where did you feel it in your body?

Section 2

Knowing Our Worth

Our Amazing Bodies
Our Worth is Constant
Empowering Ourselves

Lesson 4: Our Amazing Bodies

Connection

What have you heard people saying about their bodies or other people's bodies? What have you seen in commercials or shows? Are they true?

Discussion

The appearance or abilities of our physical bodies have nothing to do with our worth. They are miraculous containers enabling us to live on this planet. Everyone has one, and they are all good. You don't get to choose your body but you do get to choose how you carry it and treat it.

Affirmation : *My body is good as it is.*

Practice

Yes / No Embodiment
Circle up, get comfy, close eyes or focus on a center object. Imagine a YES - doing something that you love, where do you feel it in your body? What does it feel like? Now imagine a NO - something you don't want that you have the power to stop, where do you feel it in your body? What does it feel like?

Posture Activity
Everyone who is able can stand up. Instruct kids to hold posture…
- Like a superhero
- Like someone who is shy
- Like a bodybuilder
- Like a supermodel
- Take kids' suggestions

Journal Activity

Draw a picture of yourself in your favorite clothes. Emphasize your favorite features. List three of your favorite body features. What do you love about them? What do they help you do? What can you do to honor and care for your body this week?

More room to doodle!

Journal Activity

Draw a picture of yourself in your favorite clothes. Emphasize your favorite features. List three of your favorite body features. What do you love about them? What do they help you do? What can you do to honor and care for your body this week?

Lesson 5: Our Worth is Constant

Connection

Does anyone want to share something you see as a flaw about yourself? (Leaders can start with their own example.) How can you use this to help others?

Discussion

It is common to compare ourselves to others. Sometimes we think that doing something that others can't do or being something that others can't be mean we hold more worth than them. The truth is, no matter how great we are at something, comparing ourselves to others will never satisfy our desire to know our worth. Even the most powerful and popular people in the world struggle with believing their worth.

The things that we consider to be our flaws actually help us grow empathy for others. Our struggles are a big part of our purpose. They can help us be more supportive to people going through similar things.

Affirmation : *My worth is constant*

Practice

Birthday Cake Breath
Because you're just as precious as the day you were born. Hold hand(s) in front of your mouth, extend the correct amount of fingers (Candles) flickering. Inhale and blow out each candle one by one..

Mindful Minute
1. Focus on the center object or close your eyes.
2. Focus on breathing in and out a little slower than usual.
3. Your mind will wander. When your mind wanders, congratulate yourself silently for noticing that your mind is wandering, and gently bring your focus back to your breath.
Repeat as necessary.

Journal Activity

Draw a picture of yourself as a newborn baby, write underneath it your full name, and the sentence: My worth is constant. Additionally, you can write what that baby will need in order to feel loved and supported as they grow.

My Worth is Constant

Journal Activity

Draw a picture of yourself as a newborn baby, write underneath it your full name, and the sentence: My worth is constant. Additionally, you can write what that baby will need in order to feel loved and supported as they grow.

Lesson 6: Empowering Ourselves

Connection

Have you ever wanted something that wasn't easy to get? What did you do about it?

Discussion

Sometimes we feel like we have no power. We may feel helpless or believe that we will never achieve what we want. It's true that we don't have control over lots of things in life. However, no matter what else is happening, we can always control something.
Identify your wish, want, or desire. "I want to run a marathon."

1. Identify the **feeling** you'll have when it happens. "Athletic, accomplished, special, celebrated."
2. State that feeling as a goal. "My goal is to feel athletic…"
3. List 3 actions you can take to achieve that goal.

Affirmation: *I can take steps toward any goal.*

Practice

Lion's Breath
Place your thumbs on your ears and open your hands wide to resemble a lion's mane. Take a deep breath in and stick your tongue out and ROAR as you breath out. Lion's breath releases frustration and reminds us of our power.

Mindful Minute
Focus on the center object or close your eyes.
Focus on breathing in and out a little slower than usual.
Your mind will wander. When your mind wanders, congratulate yourself silently for noticing that your mind is wandering, and gently bring your focus back to your breath. Repeat as necessary.

Journal Activity

Write or draw an action plan to achieve something meaningful to you using the steps below.
1. Identify your wish, want, or desire. "I want to run a marathon."
2. Identify the **feeling** you'll have when it happens. "I will feel 'athletic, accomplished, special, celebrated.'"
3. State that feeling as a goal. "My goal is to feel athletic…"
4. List 3 actions you can take to achieve that goal.

More room to doodle!

Journal Activity

Write or draw an action plan to achieve something meaningful to you using the steps below.
1. Identify your wish, want, or desire. "I want to run a marathon."
2. Identify the **feeling** you'll have when it happens. "I will feel 'athletic, accomplished, special, celebrated.'"
3. State that feeling as a goal. "My goal is to feel athletic…"
4. List 3 actions you can take to achieve that goal.

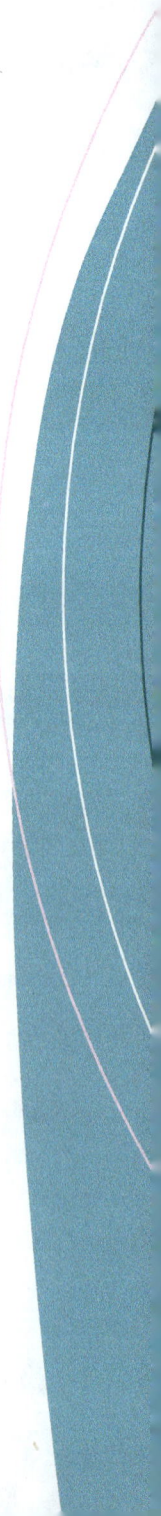

Section 3

Our Influences

Our People
Society
Our Stories

Lesson 7: Our People

Connection

What do you hear people at home saying often? How about at school? Have kids volunteer messages they've heard repeated at home and at school. What are those messages about? Are they positive or negative? Are they fear-based or love-based?

Discussion

The messages people repeat show their values. How you feel about yourself and what you believe is partly from messages you receive in your home and school. These may affect if we feel good or bad about ourselves. No matter how much we may agree or disagree with these messages, they influence our beliefs. We can disagree with people at home, and still know that they love us the best way they know how. And we can choose people we trust from all sorts of places to be our chosen family.

Affirmation: *No matter what, somebody loves me.*
No matter what, I am loved.

Practice

Somatic Boundary
Stand in a circle, have ample space to move your arms.
Stand with your feet shoulder-width apart. Lift your hands and push them
away from you, holding your hands out in front of you for 3 seconds as you
say "NO" calmly and firmly. Repeat this practice 3 times.

Journal Activity

Support pyramid. Write your name at the top of the pyramid (on the next page). Write or draw your support people in the boxes below.

neighbors	family outside your home	family at home
friend	counselor	coach
teacher	pets	others?

Write or draw yourself in the top triangle. Now write the people, pets, and things that support you in each brick below.

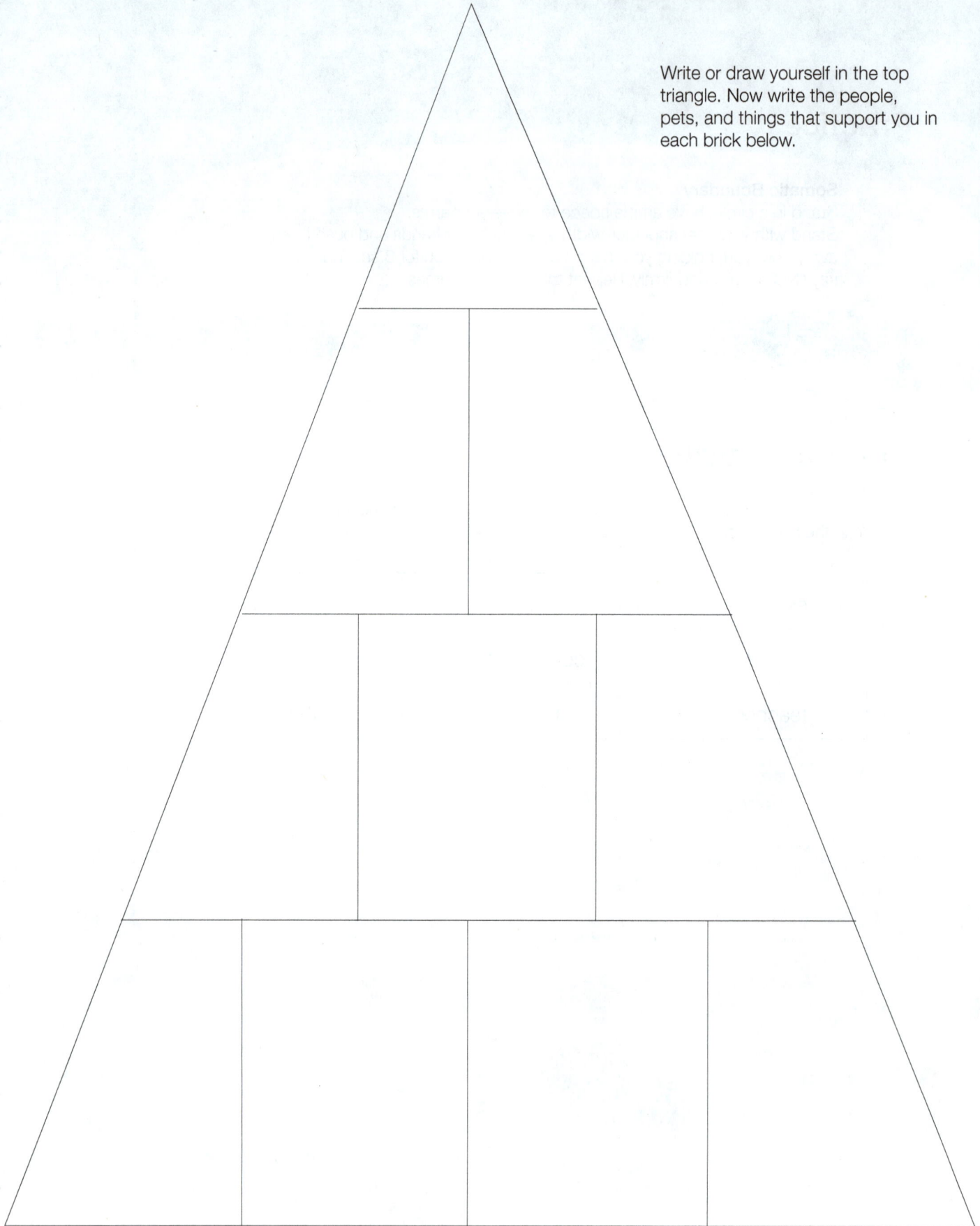

Journal Activity

Support pyramid. Write your name at the top of the pyramid. Write or draw your support people in the boxes below.

neighbors	family outside your home	family at home
friend	counselor	coach
teacher	pets	others?

Lesson 8: Our Society

Connection

What TV shows do you watch? What messages do they send about what's valued? What commercials stick out in your mind? What were the values they emphasized? What about the values emphasized in school? How might any of these have influenced your beliefs or how you feel about yourself?

Discussion

Yesterday we talked about our family and other close support people and their influence on us. Today we are going to look at messages we receive through advertisements, laws, movies, and streaming. Our brains are constantly receiving information from the media about what to think, and believe, what's important, and what's not. These messages can make us feel good or bad about ourselves. Let's look at some of those messages and decide which we want to keep believing.

Affirmation: *I choose what to believe. I don't have to believe all the messages I receive.*

Practice

Spiderman Breathing
(Option #1) Sit on the floor (but can also be done walking). Place palms facing up on your knees. Bring your ring and middle finger in so that they touch your palms. With each breath open your hands, with each exhale, bring in your ring and middle finger.

(Option #2) Inhale and bring closed hands palm in and hold at chest. Exhale, pretending you are shooting webbing from your hands to the wall or ceiling.

Mindful Minute
1. Focus on the center object or close your eyes.
2. Focus on breathing in and out just a little slower than usual.
3. Your mind will wander. When your mind wanders, congratulate yourself silently for noticing that your mind is wandering, and gently bring your focus back to your breath. Repeat as necessary.

Journal Activity

Write or draw what your own society would be like. What messages would you send to kids to help them develop healthy self-esteem?

More room to doodle!

Journal Activity

Write or draw what your own society would be like. What messages would you send to kids to help them develop healthy self-esteem?

Lesson 9: Our Stories

Connection

What's something you may have said to yourself when you got a bad grade? When you made a mistake? Got picked last for a team? When your grown-ups are upset with you? Can you think of any self-messages that you think about yourself often? How do they make you feel?

Discussion

So far this week we've talked about our bodies, our families and support people, and messages from society. Everyone is influenced by these messages, and they influence how we talk to ourselves. Today we are going to practice listening to ourselves and pay attention to what we're telling ourselves.

Affirmation: *I can be a source of kindness to myself.*

Practice

Breathwork
Ocean Breathing: Cup each ear with a hand and breathe deeply in and out.

Mindful Minute
1. Focus on the center object or close your eyes.
2. Focus on breathing in and out just a little slower than usual.
3. Your mind will wander. When your mind wanders, congratulate yourself silently for noticing that your mind is wandering, and gently bring your focus back to your breath. Repeat as necessary.

Journal Activity

Write or draw a word that describes your most common self-message. How does that compare with how you'd talk to a friend? Now write 3-5 messages you could send yourself that would feel good to hear. Choose your favorite one and write it somewhere you'll see it every day.

More room to doodle!

Journal Activity

Write or draw a word that describes your most common self-message. How does that compare with how you'd talk to a friend? Now write 3-5 messages you could send yourself that would feel good to hear. Choose your favorite one and write it somewhere you'll see it every day.

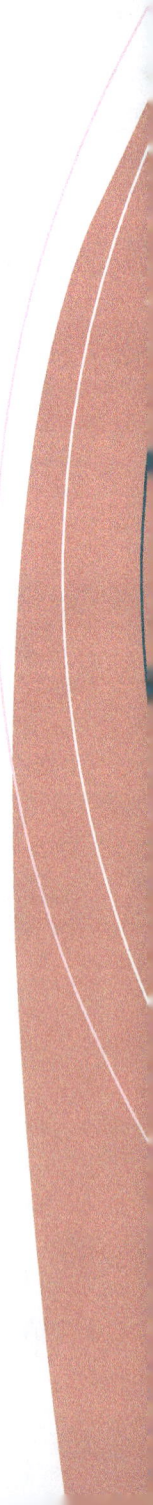

Section 4

Self-Compassion

Affirmations
Joy-mapping
Gratitude is a Super Power

Lesson 10: Affirmations

Connection

Raise your hand if you are:
- Brave
- A good listener
- Kind to animals
- Funny
- Grateful
- A good friend
- Honest
- Kind to people
- Talented
- Generous
- Hardworking
- Energetic

*Now raise your hand and tell me a good quality you have that wasn't listed.

Discussion

Today we are going to discover and embrace our positive qualities. Every single person on the planet, no matter who they are, what they do, or where they're from, brings something important and good to this planet. People can point out your positive qualities, but no one can make you believe them. That's your job!

Go around the circle, and each person says a good quality about the person to their left. It can be anything, but it has to be something. Mentors go first to set an example.

Affirmation: *I can be a source of kindness to myself.*

Practice

Breathwork
Baby You're a Firework
Press hands flat together in front of the heart (the fireworks). As you inhale, hands lift up the center of your body until your arms are up above your head. CLAP. Then exhale with your fingers sparkling as you bring your hands back down.

Mindful Minute
1. Focus on the center object or close your eyes.
2. Focus on breathing in and out just a little slower than usual.
3. Your mind will wander. When your mind wanders, congratulate yourself silently for noticing that your mind is wandering, and gently bring your focus back to your breath. Repeat as necessary.

Journal Activity

Make your own Affirmation. An affirmation is a short positive, present, and personal phrase that we can repeat over and over until we believe it. Start with "I AM… I CAN…"

Examples: "I am safe, I can stay calm." "I am strong, I can do it."

More room to doodle!

Journal Activity

Make your own Affirmation. An affirmation is a short positive, present, and personal phrase that we can repeat over and over until we believe it. Start with "I AM… I CAN…"
Examples: "I am safe, I can stay calm." "I am strong, I can do it."

Lesson 11: Joy Mapping

Connection

Raise your hand if you like:

- Time with pets
- Restaurants
- Dancing
- Shopping
- Writing
- Music
- Singing
- Camping
- Being outside
- Reading
- Video games
- Drawing
- Making crafts
- A clean room
- Movies
- Youtube

Discussion

We can learn a lot about ourselves by looking at our likes and dislikes. Some of our likes come from our experiences, and some come from our biology - we're just born that way. Everyone has different preferences, these are things that make us unique. The more aware we are of our likes, the easier it is to make choices that bring us joy and help us cope with a bad day.

Affirmation: *Doing things that make me happy is important.*

Practice

Mindful Minute
1. Focus on the center object or close your eyes.
2. Focus on breathing in and out just a little slower than usual.
3. Your mind will wander. When your mind wanders, congratulate yourself silently for noticing that your mind is wandering, and gently bring your focus back to your breath. Repeat as necessary.

Journal Activity

JOY MAP
On the journal activity page, make a mind map of things that bring you joy.

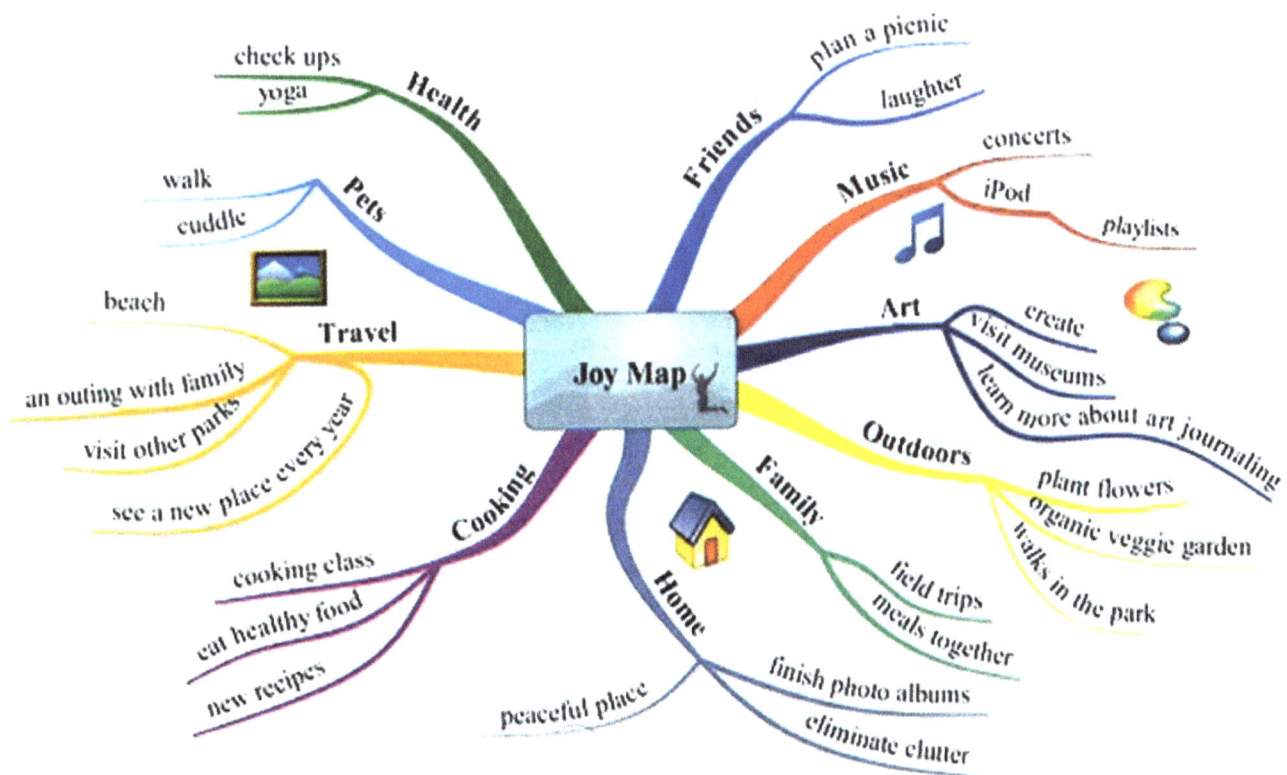

More room to doodle!

Journal Activity

63

Write or draw your best day ever. Include everything you love to do. What do your choices tell you about yourself? Now make a plan to do one of those things this week.

Lesson 12: Gratitude is a Super Power

Connection

What 3 things are you grateful for in this moment? (If it's hard to come up with ideas, think about any food you've eaten, any amount of sleep you got last night, or a nice comment you received.)

Discussion

Gratitude, thinking of things that we're happy about or thankful for, is a habit that we can develop. Lots of research shows that gratitude has crazy benefits. Science shows that when we practice gratitude:
1. We're less likely to take things for granted (awareness).
2. It reinforces generous behavior (improves friendships).
3. Directs our focus to experiences vs. things (more engaged).
4. Makes us feel more secure and connected.
5. Serotonin, and oxytocin (happy chemicals) surge and last longer.
6. Boosts immunity - we heal faster from injury and sickness.

Next Level: scientifically proven practices to improve your life:
1. 20 minutes a week writing a thank you letter to someone. (Research shows the changes to the brain from this activity are "profound" and "long-lasting.")
2. Recall a positive experience and write every detail about it. (Try doing this every day for 21 days.)
3. Write or draw 3 things you're grateful for that happened in the last 24 hours.

Affirmation: *I can be grateful for something at all times.*

Practice

Rocket Breathing
Press hands flat together (the capsule), in front of the heart, placing elbows (the engines) on the floor. Breathe in, and as you inhale the rocket takes off (up the center of your body until your arms are up above your head, and exhale back down so that the elbows land back on the earth). Repeat.

Happy Freeze Dance
Play music for the kids to dance to, shut it off randomly, and they have to freeze when the music stops. This activity works great for younger students.

Journal Activity

Write or Draw to finish the sentences.
I am grateful for …
I feel lucky because…
Something I will always be thankful for is …
One thing I really appreciate is…

More room to doodle!

More room to doodle!

Journal Activity

Write or Draw to finish the sentences.

I am grateful for …

I feel lucky because…

Something I will always be thankful for is …

One thing I really appreciate is…

Section 5

Spreading Compassion

The Power of Words
Bucket Filling
Empathy

Lesson 13: The Power of Words

Connection

Everyone can share a word that they really like and explain why they like it, or you can start with the videos referenced on page 73.

Discussion

Have you ever heard that every word casts a spell? That's why they call it SPELLING. Words express intentions, and the more they are expressed, the more likely they will become reality. So choose what you say carefully, especially what you say to yourself! Words are powerful.

Plant project transcription: The store IKEA did an experiment where they took two identical plants and invited students to compliment one and bully the other every day for a week. They were both given the same amount of light and water. The bullied plant wilted and the complimented plant stayed healthy. This experiment was repeated at a middle school and got the same results.

Water Experiment transcription: A scientist named Masaru Emoto exposed different containers of water to different words and music. Water exposed to uplifting words, like "Thank you" formed beautiful geometric crystals. But water exposed to, "you fool" and other degrading words resulted in deformed crystals, like that of polluted water.

Affirmation: *My words hold power.*

Practice

Favorite Word
Ask each student to share a kind word that they love and why it's meaningful to them.

Baby, You're a Firework
Press hands flat together in front of your heart (the fireworks). Breathe in, and as you inhale the firework takes off (up the center of your body until your arms are up above your head. CLAP. Then exhale out, with your fingers sparkling downward to be the exploding fireworks. Repeat. If you can, play the song during this exercise.

Journal Activity

Create our own Word of Intention. Write it carefully and decorate the word. Word ideas: Fun, laughter, joy, rest, swimming, party, friends, family, health, love, calm, fair, inclusion.

Additional Activity: Watch short videos about these experiments

Plant project Student's Science Project Experiments On Bullying Plants (www.cbsnews.com/newyork/news/bullied-plants-project-bullying-samantha-petraglia-long-island-coalition-against-bullying/)

Water Experiment: Masaru Emoto's Experiment in Gratitude (secretofwaterthemovie.com)

More room to doodle!

Journal Activity

Create our own Word of Intention. Write it carefully and decorate the word. Word ideas: Fun, laughter, joy, rest, swimming, party, friends, family, health, love, calm, fair, inclusion.

Lesson 14: Bucket Filling

Connection

Can you remember a time when someone did something nice for you? Did it make you feel so happy that you wanted to do something nice, too?

Discussion

Healing, acts of kindness, and happy feelings are contagious! You may have heard of the concept of bucket filling. Imagine everyone has an imaginary bucket. Good feelings fill the bucket, and things that make us feel bad (being left out, getting yelled at, failing a test) empty the bucket. The catch is: when you fill someone else's bucket, your bucket gets filled too. And when you empty someone else's bucket, your bucket empties, too.

Optional Activity: Read "How Full is Your Bucket?" by Carol McCloud. Appropriate for kids 12 and under.

Affirmation: Filling someone else's bucket fills mine, too!

Practice

Rainstorm
Let's imagine we're filling our buckets with happy rain.
1. Rub hands together.
2. Tap hands on lap, getting faster.
3. Lightning: CLAP hands up high!
4. Thunder: STOMP feet! Now in reverse.

Journal Activity

Write or draw a time when someone filled your bucket. Now write or draw a time when you filled someone else's bucket.

More room to doodle!

More room to doodle!

Journal Activity

Write or draw a time when someone filled your bucket. Now write or draw a time when you filled someone else's bucket.

Lesson 15: Empathy

Connection

Think of a recent disagreement you've had. (Examples: mom yelled at you for forgetting to do something, or you borrowed something and lost it, or you and someone else wanted to be first in line). Now, imagine you are the other person. Consider their perspective. How might it feel to be the other person? Thinking about how the other person might feel helps us to act with compassion.

Discussion

Understanding how another person feels is called empathy. Have you ever heard the expression "walk a mile in their shoes"? It means putting ourselves in someone else's position. Empathy is a powerful tool for getting along with others. Compassion is like empathy plus kindness. It's the desire to forgive and ease someone's suffering. It is most important to be compassionate with yourself. The more compassionate we are with ourselves, the more we can be compassionate with others.

Affirmation: *Being kind to myself helps me be kind to others.*

Practice

Mindful Minute
1. Focus on the center object or close your eyes.
2. Focus on breathing in and out a little slower than usual.
3. Your mind will wander. When your mind wanders, congratulate yourself silently for noticing that your mind is wandering, and gently bring your focus back to your breath. Repeat as necessary.

Send Good Thoughts
Imagine someone you love is standing in front of you.
Say something really nice to them in your mind.
Now imagine someone else, someone you don't know as well.
Say something really nice to them in your mind.
Imagine them saying those really nice things to you.
Take a long breath in, and let it all the way out.

Journal Activity

Think of a challenge you've had recently. Now write or draw how the other person might be thinking or feeling about it.

More room to doodle!

Journal Activity

Think of a challenge you've had recently. Now write or draw how the other person might be thinking or feeling about it.

Section 6

Understanding Our Power

The Power of Diversity
Identity & Privilege
Overcoming Bias

Lesson 16: The Power of Diversity

Connection

What would happen if everyone had the same job? What if there were only one type of animal? What about if everyone had the same talents and skills? Can you think of some good things that come because people are different from one another?

Discussion

Think about how many different plants and animals exist. Through this diversity, every task in nature gets accomplished. Different organisms depend on each other to carry out their specific purpose. Each of us is designed to be uniquely ourselves. This means that we have our own path to follow. We are not created to be understood by everyone. Nobody is. And that's okay. We are supposed to be different!

Brainstorm ways people are different:
Abilities
Skin tone
Language spoken
Gender expression
Beliefs
Family structure
Likes and dislikes
Hair
What else?

Affirmation: *The world needs my unique offering.*

Practice

Make Your Own Hand Symbol

Hand symbols have been used for thousands of years to communicate and set intentions. Make the following gestures and discuss their meanings.

👍 👌 ✌️ ✊

Ask students to come up with their own unique hand symbol and give it a meaning, then share it with the group.

Mindful Minute

1. Focus on the center object or close your eyes.
2. Focus on breathing in and out a little slower than usual.
3. Your mind will wander. When your mind wanders, congratulate yourself silently for noticing that your mind is wandering, and gently bring your focus back to your breath. Repeat as necessary.

Journal Activity

Write or draw a list of 10 words that describe you best. Include the things you wish to be. Our desires and wishes are absolutely a part of who we are, and give us a clue as to what we're meant to do in the world.

More room to doodle!

Journal Activity

Write or draw a list of 10 words that describe you best. Include the things you wish to be. Our desires and wishes are absolutely a part of who we are, and give us a clue as to what we're meant to do in the world.

Lesson 17: Identity & Privilege

Connection

Earlier we discussed ways that people are different from each other. Which of your identity characteristics do you think about most often? Do you think your unique traits affect how you're treated?

Discussion

Here are some things we know about power:

- Privilege holds power.
- Most of us have some sections of identity in different levels of privilege and hold some power.
- Power comes with a lack of awareness. The closer to the center, the harder to see our privilege.
- Marginalized identities, farther outside, are in the best position to inform and make decisions that affect that section of identity.

Affirmation: All sections of my identity are important.

Practice

Identity Wheel:
Use the example on page 90 as a guide for a whiteboard drawing or make copies for groups or individuals. Write the category outside the circle, the most marginalized identity closest to the outside, and identities with increased power toward the center.

Abilities	Talents	Likes & Dislikes
Hair	Skin Tone	Language
Gender Expression	Religion	What else?

Mindful Minute
1. Focus on the center object or close your eyes.
2. Focus on breathing in and out a little slower than usual.
3. Your mind will wander. When your mind wanders, congratulate yourself silently for noticing that your mind is wandering, and gently bring your focus back to your breath. Repeat as necessary.

Journal Activity

Draw a box. Inside the box, write or draw your identities that hold privilege, according to the identity wheel. Outside the box, write down your identities that are marginalized. The identities inside the box show you where you hold privilege to spend helping identities outside the box. Your identities outside the box give you experience and knowledge to help inform identities inside the box.

Identity Wheel

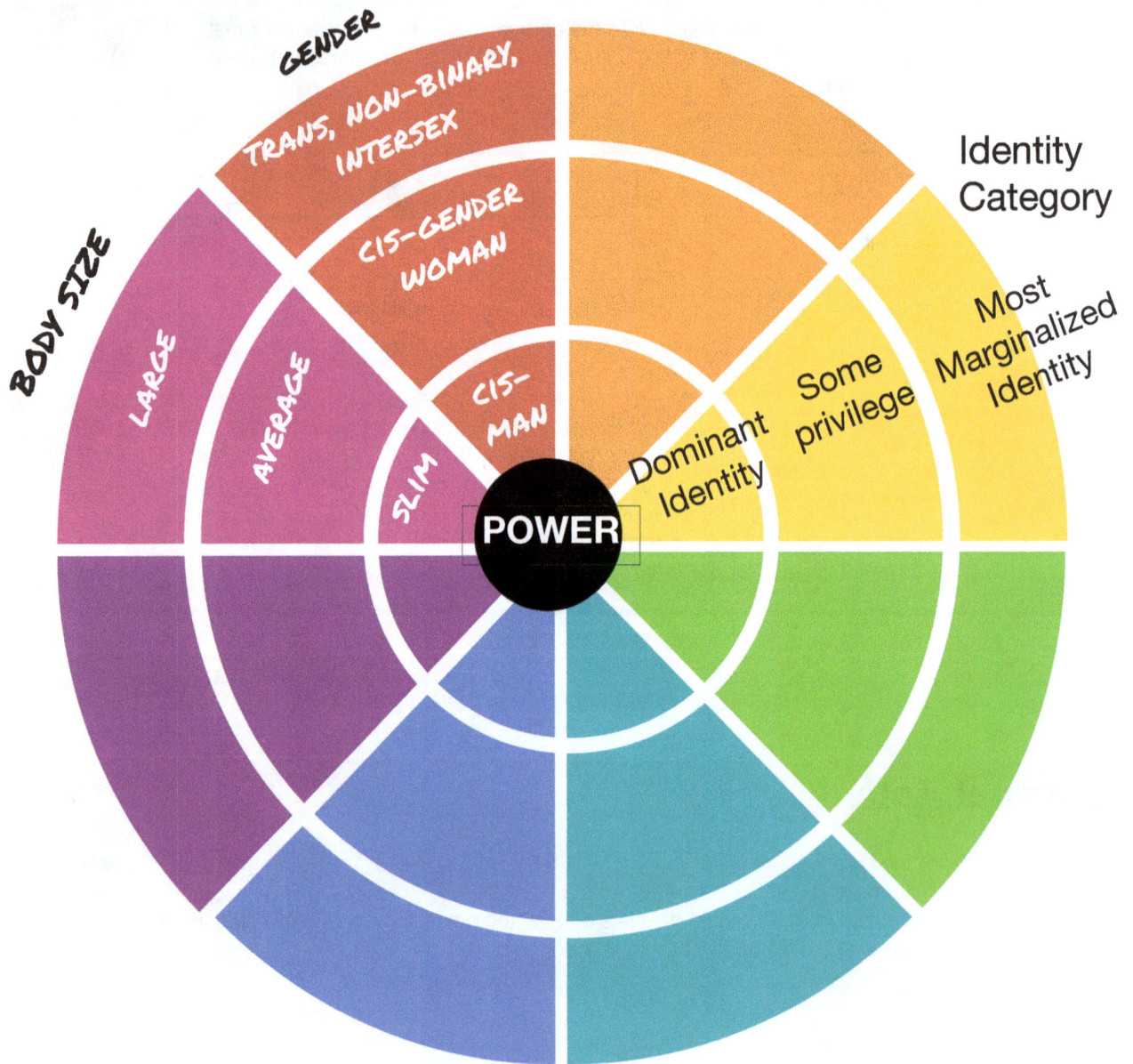

GENDER

TRANS, NON-BINARY, INTERSEX

CIS-GENDER WOMAN

CIS-MAN

BODY SIZE

LARGE

AVERAGE

SLIM

POWER

Identity Category

Most Marginalized Identity

Some privilege

Dominant Identity

Important Identity Terms to Know:

Cis-gender: Someone who identifies as the gender registered to them at birth; not transgender or nonbinary.

Nonbinary: Someone who identifies with both genders or no gender, who doesn't identify as male or female.

Trans or transgender: Someone who does not identify with the gender registered to them at birth.

Gender expression: The way a person expresses their identity, usually through how they dress. This is different than gender or attraction.

LGBTQ+: An acronym for Lesbian, Gay, Bi-sexual (attracted to both genders), Trans, Queer/Questioning + all the other identities under this umbrella. Any person that is attracted to or identifies as a gender that is outside of the dominant culture.

Identity Wheel

We can leverage (use) our privilege by:
- Asking for support from those with more power
- Offering ongoing support to those with less power
- Listening to and believing other people's lived experiences.

Journal Activity

Draw a box. Inside the box, write or draw your identities that hold privilege, according to the identity wheel. Outside the box, write down your identities that are marginalized. The identities inside the box show you where you hold privilege to spend helping identities outside the box. Your identities outside the box give you experience and knowledge to help inform identities inside the box. Here are some examples to get you started:

Lesson 18: Overcoming Bias

Connection

Bias Test

Imagine what the person looks like when I say:

Doctor	Nurse	Criminal	Lawyer
Immigrant	Judge	President	Dancer

What gender/skin tone/other physical features did you give each role?

Discussion

Bias is a shortcut the brain takes to save energy by assuming and making quick judgments. We're usually not aware of our biases, they are often wrong, and at times harmful to others. There are many different kinds of bias.

Affinity bias	We gravitate toward people who are similar to us.
Halo effect	When someone has a trait we admire, we assume they have other admirable qualities. Example: We might think a good-looking person is also intelligent and interesting.
Confirmation bias	We look for information that confirms our beliefs, and overlook opposing facts.
Implicit bias	From all the messages we receive from media and families in our lifetime, we're not even aware of it.

Bias Inventory

We can overcome bias by becoming aware and exposing ourselves to diverse perspectives. Look at your social media feeds. Could they use more diversity? We can choose to follow people in the media who have different identities and backgrounds than us. Ask students to share suggestions.

Practice

Mindful Minute
1. Focus on the center object or close your eyes.
2. Focus on breathing in and out a little slower than usual.
3. Your mind will wander. When your mind wanders, congratulate   yourself silently for noticing that your mind is wandering, and gently bring your focus back to your breath. Repeat as necessary.

Journal Activity

It's human to fall into bias, especially when we're tired, stressed, hungry, or thirsty. It's hard to see our own biases. Write or draw a few biases you think you might have. Now write one action step you can do to reduce your bias.

Check out the Stroop Test _shows how the brain tries to take shortcuts. How Fast Is Your Brain? The top rows may be easier for your brain to process because we're used to associating the colors with the words. Bias works the same way; Our brain gets used to assuming things about people based on their characteristics._

More room to doodle!

Journal Activity

It's human to fall into bias, especially when we're tired, stressed, hungry, or thirsty. It's hard to see our own biases. Write or draw a few biases you think you might have. Now write one action step you can do to reduce your bias.

Section 7

Our Resilience

Releasing Trauma
Mistakes are Inevitable
Repairing Harm

Lesson 19: Releasing Trauma

Connection

Have you ever experienced something upsetting that affected you for a long time afterward?

Discussion

Trauma is the lasting effect of a disturbing or harmful event. Trauma can happen from one big event (falling off a ladder), or from lots of little harmful events (getting picked on every day). Everybody has some trauma in their lives. Trauma can affect us physically, like a scar from a deep wound. It can also affect how we feel and behave.

Trauma can be contagious. People who've experienced lots of trauma can behave in ways that cause harm to others. For example, a school bully probably has experienced trauma. They may not have the tools to release and heal their trauma, so they try to relieve their pain by overpowering and hurting other people.

A traumatic event doesn't just impact the victim. It also increases the load of trauma and stress in the person causing the harm, and any witnesses.

Our story does not end there! Today we're going to learn how to release and heal trauma so we can stop the spread!

Practice

Trauma Release

Remember how we learned about the Chihuahua brain and the wise owl brain? Activating the wise owl brain heals. It heals the body, and the mind, and even heals behavior. All of the mindfulness tools in this course help heal trauma. A faster and more fun way to reduce the effects of trauma is to release it. The following is a list of actions that release trauma.

- Hit the air
- Stomp feet
- Sway
- Cry
- Shake
- Scream (not at someone)
- Shout - Try it now, "I RELEASE TRAUMA AND STOP THE SPREAD!"

Bunny Breath

Animals tremble to release the trauma in their bodies. Imagine a bunny is running from a fox, and narrowly escapes into the hollow of a tree. The bunny is safe but still affected by the life-threatening event, so it trembles to release the fear and trauma from its body. It's kind of the same thing you may have experienced after a long cry, when your breath feels shaky. That's your body doing a great job at regulating and releasing stress. Let's practice bunny breathing. You can put your hands out in front of your chest like paws if you want.

1. Take 4 QUICK inhales through your nose
2. Let it all out in one long exhale
3. Repeat 3 times.

Journal Activity

Journaling is also a way to release and heal trauma. Write or draw a letter to someone who you feel hurt you. Tell them all the ways it made you feel. You won't give them the letter so you don't have to worry about how they will react. (Remember that fantasizing about getting even will actually cause you more trauma, so focus on getting your feelings out.) When you're done, write or draw your favorite way to release trauma.

More room to doodle!

Journal Activity

Journaling is also a way to release and heal trauma. Write or draw a letter to someone who you feel hurt you. Tell them all the ways it made you feel. You won't give them the letter so you don't have to worry about how they will react. (Remember that fantasizing about getting even will actually cause you more trauma, so focus on getting your feelings out.) When you're done, write or draw your favorite way to release trauma.

Lesson 20: Mistakes are Inevitable

Connection

Have you ever done something you're not proud of? (Mentors might offer a personal example). Were there consequences? How did it make you feel?

Discussion

Everybody makes mistakes. Sometimes we blame ourselves for mistakes to the point that it ruins our mood for a long time. Today we are going to forgive ourselves and others for our mistakes. It's true that the better we are at forgiving ourselves, the easier it is to let go of resentment and forgive other people.

Practice

Bee Breathing
Cover your ears with your fingers. Take a deep breath in through your nose and hummmmmm out. It sounds like buzzing inside your head. If it's too loud inside your head, uncover your ears. Repeat 3 times.

Self Compassion Exercise
1. Close your eyes or stare at 1 object, put your hand to your heart, think of a difficult thing between you and another person, hand to heart, and say "Ouch!"
2. Think of others feeling the same way, notice if you feel kindness toward them and yourself.
3. Lastly, reassure yourself, "This will pass soon / I am my own ally / I accept myself and my feelings. I forgive myself and let it go."

Journal Activity

Write or draw a mistake that you made or make often that you regret. Next, write I FORGIVE YOU.

More room to doodle!

Journal Activity

Write or draw a mistake that you made or make often that you regret. Next, write I FORGIVE YOU.

Lesson 21: Repairing Harm

Connection

We've all made mistakes that hurt other people. Would anyone like to share a story where they accidentally hurt someone's feelings or body? (Leaders can start with an example.)

Discussion

The 4 Steps to Repair a Mistake

We've talked about how everyone makes mistakes. Today we're going to learn what to do when we hurt someone. This happens to everyone too, and it's an important skill, in 4 steps. Sometimes both people need to apologize, but you can only control what you do, they are on their own journey.

1. **Self-Reflection** - First find calm by doing the mindful minute, shaking your body, or another tool to activate the wise owl brain. Imagine what the other person might be experiencing. What could you have done differently?

2. **Communicating the Apology** - Name the harm you caused, and express your regret "I'm sorry for…" You can ask for forgiveness but understand that they might need more time to forgive.

3. **Repair** - The other person may have a different viewpoint than you. Try to believe their lived experience, and come up with ways to make the situation better for them. The other person might not be ready to talk or trust you. That's okay! Give them space and time. This is hard but you're doing a great job. Work on forgiving yourself in this space.

4. **Behavior Change** - Put your repair plan into action. Ask a friend to help you or make a chart in your journal to mark off once you've achieved the action.

Practice

Scenarios
In pairs or groups, come up with the 4 parts of repair for the scenarios on the following page. You can copy and hand out scenarios or enlarge and discuss them as a group.

Journal Activity

Think of a time when you made a mistake that hurt someone. Write or draw the 4 steps of an apology for that situation.

Scenario 1:
In gym, Bryce threw a basketball that hit Shane in the face. Shane got mad and threw a basketball at Bryce's face.

1. Reflect
2. Apologize for…
3. Repair Plan
4. Behavior Change

Scenario 2:
Isla was over at PJ's house. Isla asked Jenn if she could borrow the book she was reading when she was done. Jenn said no, so Isla put it in her bag when Jenn wasn't looking and took the book home.

1. Reflect
2. Apologize for…
3. Repair Plan
4. Behavior Change

Scenario 3:
Noelle and Tommy are on the trampoline. Noelle was jumping as hard as she could and Tommy was scared to be bouncing that high. Tommy cried out for Noelle to stop but she was having so much fun so she didn't stop.

1. Reflect
2. Apologize for…
3. Repair Plan
4. Behavior Change

Scenario 4:
Charlotte ate the last brownie that Sam was looking forward to. Sam called Charlotte fat for eating the brownie.

1. Reflect
2. Apologize for…
3. Repair Plan
4. Behavior Change

Journal Activity

Think of a time when you made a mistake that hurt someone. Write or draw the 4 steps of an apology for that situation.

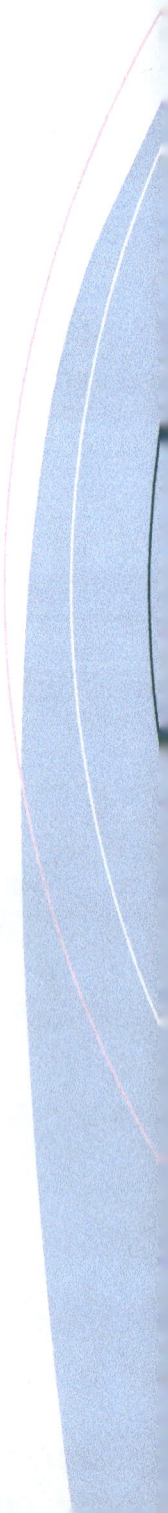

Section 8

Our Leadership

Forgiving Others
Advocating for Others
Action Plan

Lesson 22: Forgiving Others

Connection

Can you think of a time when someone made a mistake that really hurt you? What were the consequences for them?

Discussion

Last time we talked about making mistakes, practicing self-compassion, and forgiving ourselves. Today we are going to make space inside to forgive others who made mistakes that hurt us.

When we forgive others, it doesn't mean that we allow anyone to treat us badly. Carrying around resentment and anger for another person can make us mentally and physically sick. Rather, forgiveness frees us from the anger and resentment that keeps us connected to the hurt.

Everyone has ego and intuition, they're the little voices inside you. Ego's focus is to protect, and Intuition's focus is to love. If your life is a cup, Ego protects the cup, Intuition fills the cup. Sometimes our ego holds on to anger because it wants to protect us from being hurt again. Forgiving others is a skill we can develop, just like forgiving ourselves. Today we are going to practice tuning into our intuition and bringing ego into balance.

Recall some of the thoughts you've had today. Were any of them fear / protection based? That was probably your ego. Is there any thing you can say to yourself to help calm that fear or need for protection? Example: "Ego, I appreciate your looking out for me, but in this moment, I am safe, and I want to focus on having fun."

Affirmation: *I forgive myself and others to be happy and free.*

Practice

Breathwork: 123 CLAP!
Open arms wide. Count 1..2..3.. And CLAP one time. □
Rub your hands together and make some energy.
Place your hands on your belly and take a long breath in and let it out.
Repeat the first 2 steps and this time place your hands over your heart.
Long breath in, and let it alllll the way out.

Mindful Minute
1. Focus on the center object or close your eyes.
2. Focus on breathing in and out a little slower than usual.
3. Your mind will wander. When your mind wanders, congratulate   yourself silently for noticing that your mind is wandering, and gently bring your focus back to your breath. Repeat as necessary.

Journal Activity

Write or draw something that someone else did that hurt you. Next, write or draw I FREE MYSELF FROM THE HURT AND ANGER I CARRY. If you feel like you can forgive this, also write I FORGIVE.

More room to doodle!

Journal Activity

Write or draw something that someone else did that hurt you. Next, write or draw I FREE MYSELF FROM THE HURT AND ANGER I CARRY. If you feel like you can forgive this, also write I FORGIVE.

Lesson 23: Advocating for Others

Connection

Have you ever witnessed or heard a story about someone you know being treated unfairly or bullied? What did you do? What did you wish you could do?

Discussion

Sometimes people who have marginalized identities get bullied or picked on. Today we are going to practice taking action in the following scenarios. There are three ways to hold people accountable for the harm they've caused: Calling In, Calling Out, and Reporting.

CALLING IN = Privately letting someone know they did or said something hurtful.
Best to use when you have as much or more power than the person causing harm (a fellow student, a family member).
Try this first when you want to stay friendly with the person.
Likely more effective than calling out.
Takes compassion and energy.

CALLING OUT = Publicly letting someone know they said or did something hurtful.
Best to use when the person doing harm has more power than you (teachers, leaders).
Use after your attempts to call in haven't helped.
Use if public awareness of the harm will help to bring change.
Prepare for backlash.

REPORTING = Telling someone else in power.
This is best used when you don't feel safe calling in or calling out.
Use when you have a trusted adult that has the power to call in or call out on your behalf.

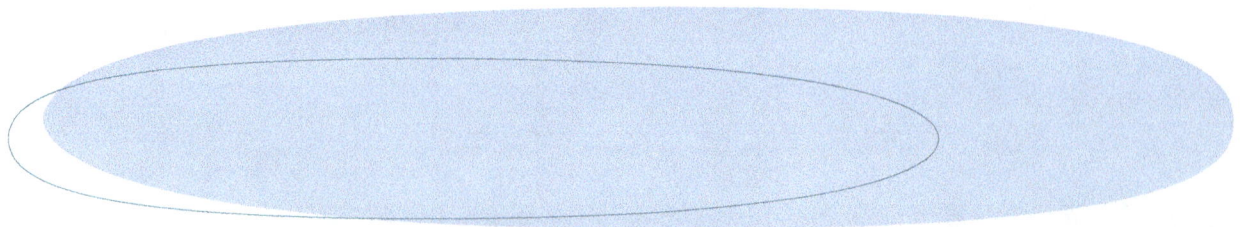

Practice

Scenarios
Discuss the scenarios on the following page as a group or in pairs. The page can be photocopied and cut so that each group has one scenario.

Mindful Minute
1. Focus on the center object or close your eyes.
2. Focus on breathing in and out a little slower than usual.
3. Your mind will wander. When your mind wanders, congratulate   yourself silently for noticing that your mind is wandering, and gently bring your focus back to your breath. Repeat as necessary.

Journal Activity

Author Ijeoa Oluo says - "When our privilege intersects with someone else's oppression, we find our opportunities to make real change."

Write or draw a statement of commitment to advocate for others the next opportunity you find. Include a phrase that you could use when needed. (Examples: Not cool, that's not funny, I like the way they look, that's not okay, everyone deserves respect.)

Call In, Call Out, or Report?
Lily's teacher refused to let her classmate Mason go to the bathroom, even after he asked several times. Mason ended up having an accident in the classroom. What should Lily do?

Who has the position of power? What are the risks of each potential action?

Call In, Call Out, or Report?
Every morning at the bus stop, Dustin sees Will get picked on by two older kids. Everyone pretends not to notice because they're scared of the bullies. On the bus, Will tells Dustin that he doesn't want to tell his parents or teacher because he's afraid that will make it worse. What could Dustin do? (This is a tricky one!)

Who has the position of power? What are the risks of each potential action?

Call In, Call Out, or Report?
In gym class, Max heard Luke call Preston a name and they started fighting. Neither of them had gotten in trouble in school before. They were sent to the principal's office. Preston, who's Black, got suspended and Luke, who's white, just got a detention. What could Max do?

Who has the position of power? What are the risks of each potential action?

Call In, Call Out, or Report?
Pam overhears her classmate Michaela calling the new student Suzi "Chinese" even though Suzi asked her to stop. She's lived in Illinois her whole life and was adopted from Korea. What could Pam do?

Who has the position of power? What are the risks of each potential action?

Journal Activity

Author Ijeoa Oluo says - "When our privilege intersects with someone else's oppression, we find our opportunities to make real change."

Write or draw a statement of commitment to advocate for others the next opportunity you find. Include a phrase that you could use when needed. (Examples: Not cool, that's not funny, I like the way they look, that's not okay, everyone deserves respect.)

Lesson 24: Putting It All Into Action

Connection

What was one thing that you learned from these lessons? What did you like / not like?

Discussion

Our last lesson! Throughout this course, we've learned a lot of truths and a lot of practices to help us feel better about ourselves and help others do the same. We learned that everyone has their own talents, likes, and traits, and that we all benefit from each other's uniqueness. How can we use our talents and favorite activities to create more safe, fair, and welcoming spaces? Are there practices from this course that you'd like to continue practicing? Brainstorm a plan to keep it going.

Optional Activities
Read "I Can Do Hard Things" by Gabi Garcia.
Celebration Dance- This works well with younger students.

How to: You may already have a dance routine for your classroom. If not, just put on some music, and start moving your bodies! Turning it into a game like freeze dance— where someone randomly turns the music off and everyone has to freeze—may elicit more participation.

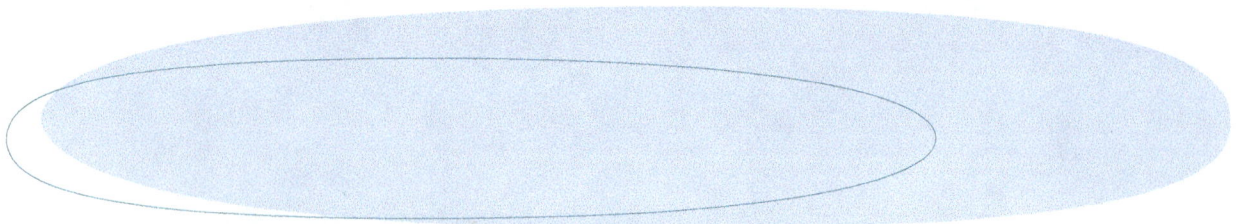

Practice

Give each student the opportunity to finish this sentence. I'm proud of myself because _____.

Mindful Minute
1. Focus on the center object or close your eyes.
2. Focus on breathing in and out a little slower than usual.
3. Your mind will wander. When your mind wanders, congratulate   yourself silently for noticing that your mind is wandering, and gently bring your focus back to your breath. Repeat as necessary.

Journal Activity

In this course, we learned that taking care of ourselves helps us feel better. And when we feel good, we can help others better. Write or draw 1- 3 things that you can do (from this course or your own ideas) to make yourself and your school safe, fair, and welcoming.

More room to doodle!

Journal Activity

In this course, we learned that taking care of ourselves helps us feel better. And when we feel good, we can help others better. Write or draw 1- 3 things that you can do (from this course or your own ideas) to make yourself and your school safe, fair, and welcoming.

Thank You

It's been a dream come true to partner with you in creating more inclusive spaces inside and out through this curriculum. I hope that it served you and your students well.

We would love your feedback!
You can reach us at:
www.bravespaceconsulting.com
www.facebook.com/bravespace
www.instagram.com/bravespace_co

If you would consider writing a review on Amazon, I would be so grateful. Scan the QR Code below to go write your review on Amazon.

APPENDIX I.

Breathwork Options from www.mindfulartssf.org

1. **Starfish (Take Five/Five Finger) Breathing:** Trace your hand with a finger, with each up or down movement, inhale or exhale.

2. **Ocean Breathing:** Cup each ear with a hand and breathe deeply in and out.

3. **Elephant Breathing:** Hold your hands in your lap, with your thumbs resting next to each other. With each inhale raise your thumbs up, with your exhale bring them back down to rest. Option: Sitting or standing with each inhale, raise your arms to the sky, and on the exhale back down to your lap. Or hold a hand of classmates, and thumb breathe together as you walk in a circle or down the hall.

4. **Spiderman Breathing:** (Option #1) Sit on the floor (but can also be done walking). Place palms skyward on your knees. Bring your ring and middle finger in so that they touch your palms. With each breath open your hands, and with each exhale, bring in your ring and middle finger. (Option #2) Inhale and bring closed hands palm in and hold at chest. Exhale, pretending you are shooting webbing from your hands to the wall or ceiling.

5. **Quiet Coyote Breathing:** Hold up your hand in the air like a quiet coyote. With each belly breath, slowly drop your thumb to create the look of a breathing coyote. Exhale. Repeat.

6. **Butterfly Breathing:** Option #1: Clasp your hands together like you are begging, trying to also get your forearms and elbows to touch. Squeeze your hands and arms together, and breathe out. On the inhale, keeping hands clasped & slightly under your chin, lift your elbows a bit above your shoulders. On the exhale, bring your elbows down so they touch again. Repeat. Option #2: Standing or sitting, on the inhale, bring both arms up alongside your body. On the exhale, lower your arms. Repeat.

7. **Shark Fin Breathing:** In a seated position, place your hand in front of your face like a shark fin. As you lower your hand to your heart say to yourself: "Sit Straight, Sit Still, Sit Silently, Softly Breathe." "I have the power to make wise decisions." Repeat.

8. **Smell a Rose, Blow Out a Candle.** Repeat.

9. **Blowfish Breathing:** Cup your mouth with your hands, like a mask. With each inhale open your hands like gills. Repeat.

10. **Balloon Breathing:** Put your hands on your belly with your fingertips together, like you're holding a breathing ball. Fill up your belly with air. As you inhale, see if you can separate your fingers, as you exhale, your fingers will come back to touch.

11. **Elevator Breathing** (Breathing Buddies): Laying down, have kids see how big they can make their bellies, with each breath. For more fun, place a breathing buddy (a stuffed animal) on their bellies to see how high they can get their buddy to go up. Limit the number of floors to 3, 4, or 5 depending on age.

12. **Rocket Breathing:** Press hands flat together (the capsule), in front of the heart placing elbows (the engines) on the floor. Breathe in, and as you inhale the rocket takes off (up the center of your body until your arms are up above your head), exhale back down so that the elbows land back on the earth. Repeat.

13. **Firecracker Breathing:** Press hands flat together in front of the heart (the fireworks). Breathe in, and as you inhale the rocket takes off (up the center of your body until arms are up above your head. CLAP. Then exhale out, with your fingers sparkling downward to be the exploding fireworks. Repeat.

14. **Crocodile Breathing:** Arms out straight, hands together (right arm above left). Breathe in big and deep while raising your right arm, exhale all at once, and close the crocodile's mouth.

15. **Beach Ball Breathing:** Big breath while opening arms wide and then overhead they come together, slowly - as if against resistance - push (hands rest on top of each other) as if pushing a beach ball underwater, while exhaling.

16. **Flower Breathing:** Begin in child's pose (curled up, knees bent, forehead on the floor), inhaling and rising up onto the knees extending arms and face up to the sky like a flower opening up in the sun, exhaling reversing back into child's pose arms by side (curling up like a flower in the evening time).

17. **Buzzing (Bumble) Bee Breathing**: Buzzing on the out-breath (Bzzzzzzz….), sucking in honey on the in-breath. Repeat. A fantastic way to bring the energy of a class down.

18. **Dragon Breathing**: Breathe in while making dinosaur hands, exhale fire out, and bring hands down.

19. **Water Faucet Breathing**: Put your arms outstretched, sides of fists touching. Squeeze hands tight and breathe in, exhale, and release fingers, sprinkling water down making a shhhhh sound. Repeat.

20. **4-7-8 Breathing**: Breath in for 4, hold for 7, and breathe out for 8. Repeat.

21. **Birthday Cake Breath**: Roll dice to see how many birthday candles you will blow out. Hold hand(s) in front of your mouth, and extend the correct amount of fingers (candles) flickering. Inhale and blow on candles until they are all out. Repeat. Roll the dice again.

22. **Incredible Hulk Breath**: On the in-breath, bring your arms up like you are flexing your muscles. On the out-breath bring your arms down slightly, releasing fists slightly, and gently bend your knees.

23. **Superman Breath**: Inhale and bring closed hands to your waist, chest up high. Exhale and bring hands down and out and up and away. I like to say, "Fly to the moon." Repeat.

24. **Wonder Woman (or Cowboy) Breath**: Inhale and bring one hand over your head, pretending to spin a lasso. Exhale and pretend to throw the lasso. Repeat.

25. **Dolphin Breath**: Hold palms together at your belly. Inhale and raise hands to your heart. Exhale and pretend to dive into the water. Repeat.

26. **Snake Breath**: Hold your hands together in front of your chest, in a prayer position. Inhale and when exhaling, wiggle your hands and arms together upwards, making the "SSSSSSS" sound. Repeat.

27. **Square Breath (Or Triangle, Rectangle, or Circle)**: Hold your pointer finger up, facing away from you. As you draw the lines of the square, breathe in and out. Inhale one line, exhale the next, inhale, exhale. Repeat.

28. **Bubble Gum Breath**: Pretend you are chewing a big piece of gum, eventually take a deep breath in through your nose. Put your hands on either side of your mouth. On the exhale, pretend your hands are the bubble gum, with each exhale allow the bubble to get bigger and bigger. Eventually, bring your hands together with a "clap", rub your hands together, and begin again.

29. **Flower of Gratitude Breathing**: Hold hands upright on your knees, or on the desk, like two closed flowers. With each exhale, think of something or someone that you are grateful for. Your fingers represent 10 petals, by the end of the 10th out breath you will have opened all 10 fingers in gratitude. On the 11th breath, bring your hands to your heart. Breathe deeply 3 times. Share with the group one thing that you are grateful for.

30. **May I be Kind Breathing**: Wrap hands together, thumbs laying side by side, then put hands on your heart and say: "May I have a kind heart." Breathe. Then up to your lips (chin). "May I have kind words. " Breathe. Then up to your forehead. "May I have kind thoughts." Breathe.

31. **KFC Breathing**: Have students silently say to themselves "May I be Kind, (breathe), May I be Focused, (breathe), May I be Calm (breathe). Especially useful during focus time, when students find focusing on their breath too challenging. Option 2: Go around the circle, each child saying only one of the phrases, their neighbor saying the next, and so on. Begin again, until you go all around the way around the circle.

32. **Cupid's Bow Breathing**: Think of someone to send loving kindness or healing to. Stretch arms towards the sky, knuckles together. Pull one fist back towards your chest, while breathing in deeply. Then breathe out, making a whooshing sound back towards the outstretched fist. Sprinkle hands down around the person you are imagining.

1. If I could go back and whisper something to myself as a little one, it would be …
2. I feel powerless when …
3. I wish I would have said …
4. I wish I felt confident enough to …
5. It makes my blood boil when…
6. I feel so …
7. I need …
8. I really want to forgive …
9. I release …
10. I no longer need/want to …
11. I daren't even admit this to myself, but …
12. I wish I could change …
13. I hate …
14. The secrets about me that nobody knows are …
15. I don't even like admitting this to myself but …
16. I feel angry, but underneath that feeling I can also feel …
17. They made me believe that …
18. I still believe that I have to …(eg: in order to be loved / accepted)
19. … that triggers me today, reminds me of … in the past
20. What needs of mine haven't been met?
21. I don't feel validated because …
22. What patterns in my adult life mirror my childhood?
23. What patterns in my adult life mirror my parents' patterns?
24. I totally avoid feeling …
25. It really hurt me when … it made me feel …
26. I know I didn't react at the time but … made me so angry
27. I wish I was brave enough to say this to your face …
28. I've never felt so low before when …
29. When you treat me like … it makes me feel …
30. Because I don't have … in my life I feel …
31. I'm scared of … because it feels like it means …
32. When I was little I felt like …when I was told …
33. Honestly, what's really making me sad right now is …
34. I cannot accept the fact that …
35. I am embarrassed by …
36. I feel at fault for …
37. I wish I was brave enough to …
38. I always feel tearful when I think about …
39. My biggest trigger right now is …
40. The words I wish I could hear from …are…
41. If I'm completely honest, I have always felt …
42. I am so ashamed that I …
43. I'm trying so hard to keep the peace about … when I would rather …
44. Write a letter to someone who hurt you (eg: a parent, a friend, a teacher, etc.) you will never send it and you can win every argument you like, let them have all your unfiltered emotion, and don't censor anything.
45. Imagine you're sitting in front of the person that hurt you, but they're not able to respond, they can only listen to you (your writing or your voice if you want to do this out loud). Let them have it.
46. Write a list of things you wish others knew about you.
47. Write a list of your secrets.
48. Make a list of everything you'd like to say yes to.
49. Make a list of everything you'd like to say no to.

50.   Make a list of things that you fear.

Journal prompts for gratitude and self-compassion

1. Think of myself as a baby version of me, hold that visualization in my mind, and list 5 things I will do today to show myself love and compassion.
2. What can I do today that I didn't think I could do a year ago?
3. What is surprising to me about myself lately that I like?
4. What happened today that I appreciate?
5. Make a list of people that I appreciate.
6. What am I most grateful for today? List at least 5 things and write about how they make me feel, no matter how small.

Important Identity Terms to Know:

Cis-gender: Someone who identifies as the gender registered to them at birth; not transgender or nonbinary.

Nonbinary: Someone who identifies with both genders or no gender, who doesn't identify as male or female.

Trans or transgender: Someone who does not identify with the gender registered to them at birth.

Gender expression: The way a person expresses their identity, usually through how they dress. This is different than gender or attraction.

LGBTQ+: An acronym for Lesbian, Gay, Bi-sexual (attracted to both genders), Trans, Queer/Questioning + all the other identities under this umbrella. Any person that is attracted to or identifies as a gender that is outside of the dominant culture.

Bibliography and Resources

For more activities and inspiration:

This Book is Anti-racist by Tiffany Jewell
The Bully Free Classroom by Allen L Bean, Ph.D.
How to Be Bully Free Workbook by Allen L Bean, Ph.D.
The 8 Keys to End Bullying Activity Book by Signe Whitson
Calm Mindfulness for Kids by Wynne Kinder M. Ed.
The Self-esteem Workbook for Teens by Lisa M Schab, LCSW
The Stress Reduction Workbook for Teens by Gina M Biegel, MA LMFT
The Yoga Pretzels Deck by Tara Guber and Leah Kalish
Breathe Like a Bear by Kira Willey
Thriving with ADHD Workbook for Kids by Kelli Miller, MSW
Anger Management Workbook for Kids by Samantha Snowden, MA
Planting Seeds by Tich Nat Hahn

Read aloud books to enhance the curriculum for elementary age:

How Full is Your Bucket? For Kids by Tom Rath and Mary Reckmeyer
Change Sings by Amanda Gorman
Not So Different by Shane Burcaw
Not So Different by Cyana Riley
Only One You/ Nadie Como Tu by Linda Kranz
Mistakes are How I Learn by Kiara Wilson
I Can Do Hard Things by Gabi Garcia and Charity Russel
Say Something! By Peter H. Reynolds
Don't Touch My Hair by Sharee Miller

Read aloud or independent Young Adult books to enhance the curriculum for middle school age:

By Jason Reynolds: *Ghost, Lu, Sunny, Patina, Miles Morales series*
By Kwame Alexander: *The Crossover, Rebound, Booked, Solo, Swing*
By Raina Telgemeier: *Sisters, Smile, Guts, Drama, Ghosts*

Acknowledgments

Sierra Melcher and Red Thread Publishing for providing the structure I didn't know I needed in a compassionate and affirming container.

Bridget Snell for heroically coming to the rescue to format this book to be beautiful and accessible.

Shannon Sheldon for your solid feedback, fast friendship, and enthusiastic support.

Tanya Lobo for trusting me and giving me the opportunity to pilot this curriculum with the precious young people at T.O.G.E.T.H.E.R. Youth Program. And for being a consistent source of support.

Kristie Dean for so graciously bringing me into the Soul Project fold, for the opportunities to work with soulful girls and women, and for your bright light. You are a beacon.

Jenn Nieters Burt for being my girl. For encouraging me through all my venting and rabbit holes. For being fiercely protective. I love you.

Carolyn Blaine for working through conditioning with me, for seeing me, hearing me, and for being irreverent with me.

Lisa Wilde Spence for 36 years of continuous giggling and bestiehood!

Nadia Clancy for all the personal and professional support, for your friendship, and for reminding me that fun exists. I thrive in your glow!

Karen Cruz, my mom, for being ridiculously proud of me at all times no matter what.

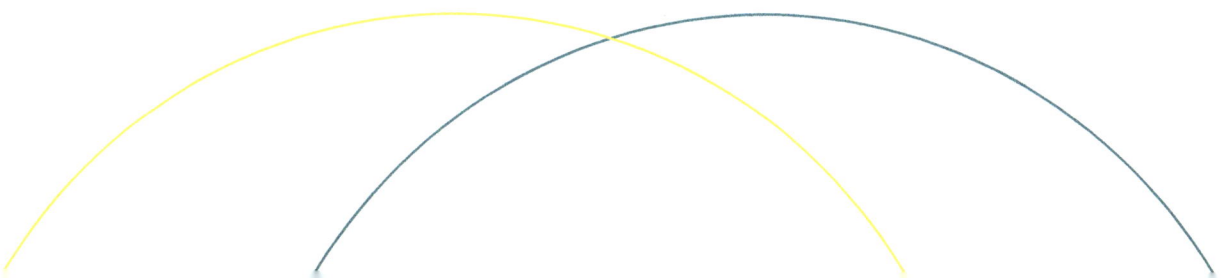

www.ingramcontent.com/pod-product-compliance
Lightning Source LLC
Chambersburg PA
CBHW052113020426
42335CB00021B/2746